To Jack,

Hope you enjoy the Squirrel Book.

Miss Doris

The Squirrel Who Was Afraid To Leave His Nest

Written by Doris Gallippi

Illustrations by Jane Wolfgang

Copyright © 2017 by Doris Gallippi
All rights reserved. No part of this book may be reproduced or transmitted in any form or by any means,
electronic or mechanical, including photocopying, recording, or by any information storage and
retrieval system, without permission in writing from the copyright owner.

ISBN: 978-0-692-94297-0

Dedication

Katie Elisabeth Rettura was the inspiration for this story. Her concerns about moving from the only home she lived in to another home with her family reminded me that making new memories is what helps us adjust to changes in our lives.

A special acknowledgment goes to my Junior Editor Taylor Nicole Rosenbaum for her contributions to the book.

This book is dedicated to my grandchildren - Katie, Nina, Chelsea, Riley, Taylor, Quinn and Ally; my step grandchildren Maddie, Liv and Char; and to all the children of parents in the United States military who must adjust to changes as their parents move from one home to another, supporting and defending America.

Boo snuggled into the curvy part of his nest.
He loved his nest.

It had a roof of leaves to keep the rain away.

On sunny days when he wanted to nap,
he would tuck himself under the shadow of the leaves
to keep the sunlight from his eyes.

Boo lived in his nest with his Mama, his Papa and his two older brothers, Buck and Barlow.

Like all fluffy-tailed baby squirrels, Boo rested while Mama and Papa Squirrel gathered seed pods and small acorns for their family to eat.

Boo's older brothers were rascals. They spent most of their time chasing each other up and down, over and under all the tree limbs in their neighborhood.

Sometimes they played the 'Topsy-Turvy' game by rolling over one another on the ground.

At night, when the moon was high above the nest, Buck and Barlow told little Boo stories about their adventures.

Early one morning while Buck and Barlow were playing on the ground, Boo decided to take a peek at them.

He crawled to the edge of his nest and looked down from the top of the tall oak tree.

"Oooh, I'M WOOZY!" he said.

Holding his tail he quickly tucked his head
into the soft fur of his mama's belly to feel safe.

Mama Squirrel was a bit worried about Boo.
She decided to have a talk with him.

She said, "Boo, sometimes it's hard to leave the place where you feel safe."

Boo looked up at her and said, "but… I know about our nest, where I eat and where my sleeping place is. I don't want anything to change."

Mama Squirrel said, "You don't want anything to change because all of your memories are in this nest."

"One day soon you will feel it is okay to leave. When you do, you will make new memories on the ground and you will feel comfortable again."

Boo spent nights worrying about what it would be like on the ground when he was away from his nest during the day. Sometimes he felt afraid. Sometimes he was unsure if he could find his way back to his nest at night to sleep with his family. And, sometimes he just worried because everything would be different.

Well…Buck and Barlow decided to help Boo in their own special way!

Early the next morning, Barlow grabbed Boo's front paw and pulled him out onto the branch of the tall tree.

Buck jumped to the tree trunk tucking himself behind Boo saying,

"You're a squirrel just like me… and we know how to climb down a tall tree."

"Hang on with your paws, Boo! Let's Go!"

"Oooooh!" said Boo as he looked down.

"This is so high…what if I fall… *I FEEL WOOZY!*"

Barlow pulled Boo's paws along the tree trunk one by one as Buck pushed from behind.

Both Mama and Papa squirrel
had a good laugh
as they heard Barlow shouting…

"Remember, you're a squirrel…you're a squirrel…you're a squirrel!"

As he climbed down the tall tree, Boo started to feel less afraid.

Before he knew it, Boo was on the ground with Mama and Papa Squirrel.
It was time for a group hug and a huge helping of tree nut treats to eat.

Draw a picture of something you remember from your other home.

Draw something you like in your new home.

**Copies Available
at
Amazon.com**

Made in the USA
Lexington, KY
01 October 2017